WAR HEADS

W9-DAZ-613

Julian Allen
Marshall Arisman
Niculae Asciu
Tony Auth
Bascove
R. O. Blechman
George Booth
Philip Burke
Seymour Chwast
Sue Coe
Paul Conrad
R. Crumb
Andrzej Dudzinski
Fritz Eichenberg
Jules Feiffer
Peter Fluck
Herb Gardner
William Garner
Luis Geronimo
Lou Grant
Sam Gross
Robert Grossman
Ron Hauge
Draper Hill
Cor Hoekstra (CORK)
Brad Holland
Frances Jetter
Edward Koren
Stephen Kroninger
Harvey Kurtzman
Roger Law
Bill Lee
David Levine
M. G. Lord
Lee Lorenz
Stan Mack

WAR HEADS

CARTOONISTS DRAW THE LINE

Edited by Steven Heller

Introduction by George Plimpton

PENGUIN BOOKS

Mark Marek
Doug Marlette
Charles E. Martin
Henry Martin
Michael Maslin
Eugene Mihaesco
Lou Myers
Pat Oliphant
Robert Osborn
David Pascal
Mike Peters
Bill Plympton
Mark Podwal
Ken Pyne
Hans Georg Rauch
Mischa Richter
Arnold Roth
Ben Sargent
Gerald Scarfe
Ronald Searle
Elwood H. Smith
Edward Sorel
Mark Alan Stamaty
Jules Stauber
Ralph Steadman
Peter Steiner
Mick Stevens
David Suter
Paul Szep
Roland Topor
John Trever
Garry Trudeau
Robert Weaver
Gahan Wilson
Don Wright
Jack Ziegler

Penguin Books Ltd, Harmondsworth,
Middlesex, England
Penguin Books, 40 West 23rd Street,
New York, New York 10010, U.S.A.
Penguin Books Australia Ltd, Ringwood,
Victoria, Australia
Penguin Books Canada Limited, 2801 John Street,
Markham, Ontario, Canada L3R 1B4
Penguin Books (N.Z.) Ltd, 182-190 Wairau Road,
Auckland 10, New Zealand

First published 1983

Copyright © American Friends Service Committee, Inc. — The Nu-
clear Weapons Freeze Campaign, 1983
Cartoons first published in this volume copyright © 1983 by Niculae
Asciu, Bascove, R. O. Blechman, Seymour Chwast, Sue Coe, Luis Ge-
ronimo, Sam Gross, Ron Hauge, Cor Hoekstra (CORK), Brad Holland,
Stephen Kroninger, Harvey Kurtzman, Bill Lee, Mark Marek, Charles
E. Martin, Michael Maslin, Eugene Mihaesco, Robert Osborn, Bill
Plympton, Mark Podwal, Ken Pyne, Mischa Richter, Elwood H. Smith,
Edward Sorel, Peter Steiner, Mick Stevens, Paul Szep, Roland Topor,
Robert Weaver, Jack Ziegler
All rights reserved

Printed in the United States of America by
R. R. Donnelley & Sons Company, Harrisonburg, Virginia

Grateful acknowledgment is made to the following contributors for car-
toons previously published and reproduced for this volume by permis-
sion. Julian Allen: Copyright © Julian Allen, 1982. Marshall Arisman:
Copyright © Marshall Arisman, 1982. Tony Auth: Copyright © Tony
Auth, 1982. George Booth: Copyright © The New Yorker Magazine,
Inc., 1976. Philip Burke: Copyright © Philip Burke, 1981. Paul Conrad:
Copyright © Los Angeles Times, 1982. R. Crumb: Copyright © R.
Crumb, 1970. Andrzej Dudzinski: Copyright © Andrzej Dudzinski,
1982. Fritz Eichenberg: Copyright © Fritz Eichenberg, 1979. Jules
Feiffer: Copyright © Jules Feiffer, 1979. Peter Fluck and Roger Law:
Front cover, "Euroshima," copyright © Peter Fluck and Roger Law,
1981. Herb Gardner: Copyright © King Features Syndicate, Inc., 1982.
William Garner: Copyright © The Commercial Appeal/United Feature
Syndicate, 1982. Lou Grant: Copyright © Oakland Tribune/Los An-
geles Times Syndicate, 1981. Robert Grossman: Copyright © Robert
Grossman, 1977. Draper Hill: Copyright © Detroit News, 1982.

Frances Jetter: Copyright © Frances Jetter, 1980. Edward Koren:
Copyright © Edward Koren, 1982. David Levine (2): Copyright
© NYREV Inc., 1979, 1981. M. G. Lord (2): Copyright © Newsday,
Inc., 1981, 1982. Lee Lorenz: Copyright © The New Yorker Maga-
zine, Inc., 1982. Stan Mack: Copyright © Stan Mack, 1982. Doug
Marlette: Copyright © Charlotte Observer, 1982. Henry Martin: Copy-
right © Punch, 1981. Lou Myers: Copyright © Lou Myers, 1980. Pat
Oliphant (2): Copyright © Universal Press Syndicate, 1982. David Pas-
cal: Copyright © David Pascal et Editions Jacques Glenat, 1975. Mike
Peters: Copyright © Dayton Daily News, 1982. Hans Georg Rauch:
Copyright © Hans Georg Rauch, 1982. Arnold Roth: Copyright
© Arnold Roth, 1982. Ben Sargent: Copyright © Austin American-
Statesman, 1981. Gerald Scarfe (2): Copyright © Gerald Scarfe, 1971,
1982. Ronald Searle: Copyright © Ronald Searle, 1981. Mark Alan Sta-
maty (2): Copyright © Mark Alan Stamaty, 1980, 1982. Jules Stauber:
Published 1980 in Die Welt ist rund by Deutscher Taschenbuch-Verlag.
Ralph Steadman: Copyright © Ralph Steadman, 1982. David Suter (2):
Copyright © David Suter, 1981, 1982. John Trever: Copyright © John
Trever, 1982. Garry Trudeau: Copyright © G. B. Trudeau, 1982; dis-
tributed by Universal Press Syndicate. Gahan Wilson: Copyright
© Playboy, 1980; reproduced by special permission from Playboy maga-
zine. Don Wright: Copyright © Miami News, 1978; syndicated by The
New York Times Syndication Sales Corp.

Many thanks to Kevin Scherzinger of the Nuclear Weapons Freeze
Campaign in New York City, the tireless organizer of the exhibition of
drawings from which this book springs. Many thanks as well to Edward
Spiro for his generosity in photographing the pieces in this exhibition and
to Michael Gifford, Estaban Perez, Albert Wehner, Gloria Sonheim,
Ann Siegel, Donna Cohn, A. P. F. Kulicke, the American Friends Service Committee, and the West-Park Presbyterian Church for their assis-
tance with the show. My gratitude goes to Lee Lorenz for his support,
to all the artists who donated their work for this very important cause,
and to Dan Weaver, the Penguin editor. —S. H.

Cover photograph by John Lawrence-Jones

Except in the United States of America, this book is sold subject to the
condition that it shall not, by way of trade or otherwise, be lent, re-sold,
hired out, or otherwise circulated without the publisher's prior consent in
any form of binding or cover other than that in which it is published and
without a similar condition including this condition being imposed on the
subsequent purchaser

Foreword

Since the early nineteenth century the bomb — from cannonball to missile — has been a unique weapon of horror in the cartoonist's arsenal against war. After the development and deployment of the atomic bomb in 1945, a new, chilling assortment of images was added to an already universal graphic vocabulary. Immediately after World War II, Robert Osborn's cautionary picture book, *War Is No Damn Good,* featured the first satiric personification of the modern bomb. During the early 1950s, after Russia built her own bomb, Herblock's diabolical, anthropomorphized H-bomb became the ultimate symbol of fear. And, in the latter part of the same decade, Jules Feiffer's prophetic cartoon exposés of the "clean-air," or neutron, bomb heightened the collective anxiety levels of his readers. Today the ICBM and MX have become part of the cartoonist's repertoire, and the nightmarish mushroom cloud is as commonplace in art as it is unthinkable in life.

Satire is the artist's corrective for a society wandering from a rational course. The ability to simplify without trivializing complex issues is the ultimate virtue of the form. It paves the way, in the public's consciousness, for more detailed and articulated arguments in favor of, in this case, a nuclear freeze.

The cartoons, caricatures, and illustrations in *War Heads* represent many approaches: from the captioned gag to visual allegory, from the editorial cartoon to the comic strip. Many of the artists employ familiar images to heighten recognition while others invent new, more personal ones. Some target political leaders because they are the creators and administrators of suicidal policies; others choose timeless imagery beyond the reach of an election or a death. These statements are different in approach, but all speak the same language, exposing the absurdity and danger of arms buildup and nuclear brinkmanship.

Many thanks go to the talented artists who have generously contributed their work to this, the first compilation of cartoons and illustrations dealing exclusively with the issue of nuclear disarmament, for the benefit of the Nuclear Weapons Freeze Campaign.

STEVEN HELLER

Introduction

David Low, the great political cartoonist for Lord Beaverbrook's *Evening Standard,* once wrote, "Without doubt, democracy often seems to need a good kick in the pants. The great point in its favor — the supreme excellence that raises it far beyond all other political systems yet conceived by the mind of man — is that you can give it one."

Perhaps of all the artisans in the practice of communication, the political cartoonist is the one best suited to provide what Low was writing about; the impact of a great political cartoon has exactly the sudden, quick, compelling force of a well-placed kick. Often the recipient cannot take it. It is no surprise that in political cultures less fortunate than democracies, the first victims of censorship are inevitably political cartoonists. A devastating combination of scorn and ridicule, coupled with skills as a draftsman, makes the political cartoonist a prime observer and chronicler, and an extremely important one, of human follies and excesses. Not only does he have the ability to reflect his times and its problems, but to a degree he also has the power to sway the public. Thomas Nast's reputation was such that on thorny political issues people would quite often say before making up their own minds, "Well, hold on now; let's wait and see what Tom makes of this."

Perhaps the most agonizing decision facing anyone in the arts is how much notice should be taken of the world outside one's own artistic sphere — how much one should apply oneself to being what the French refer to as engagé. W. H. Auden felt that the poet was of little use in this matter. Some thought that the reason he never received the Nobel Prize was because of this stance and because he had never come out against the Vietnam War. On the other hand, Ernest Hemingway, although he said that "everyone has his own conscience, and there should be no rules about how a conscience should function," went on to say that great writing invariably came out of a sense of injustice. He was explicit: "A writer without a sense of justice and of injustice would be better off editing the Year Book of a school for exceptional children."

The same can be said of the requirements of the political cartoonist. Perhaps first is wit and humor, but the second requirement is not only a sense of injustice but also truth, or at least one side of the truth.

It is very difficult to come down on the wrong side of the truth about the subject this present volume confronts. Nuclear proliferation is surely the craziest excess in the morbid history of weaponry. Military follies, their by-products, and the artifacts of war being so monstrous, caricaturing them has always been a cartoonist's preoccupation and staple. Some of the most famous cartoons we remember are concerned with these topics: Francisco Goya's *Disasters of War;* Boardman Robinson's famous and prophetic *Signed,* a death's hand signing the Versailles Treaty, with a mouse already nibbling at the document and a vulture hovering in the gloaming background; Daniel Fitzpatrick's cartoon of ant-lines of people drawing a vast gun over the horizon, titled *The Progress of Humanity;* or Charles D. Batchelor's famous cartoon implying that the folly of war repeats itself, showing a prostitute with a death's head propositioning a young European, "Come on in, I'll treat you right. I used to know your Daddy."

Batchelor, who drew for the *New York Daily News,* won the Pulitzer Prize for this cartoon in 1937. He was one of a number of winners of that award to use the topic of war. Perhaps the cartoon most pertinent to this present volume was the one that won the Pulitzer Prize in 1948. It is a drawing of an enormous atomic bomb on top of which sits a suburban home, with a birdbath, a sun umbrella, and a couple out on the patio sublimely unaware of their underpinnings — this vast bomb balancing on a precipice and tilting alarmingly above an abyss labeled "World Destruction." The drawing is by none other than Reuben Goldberg, better known by his nickname, Rube, and for the primitive layouts for his wacky inventions.

The specific subject of this book is what concerned Goldberg — the bomb — except that its first name changed from "Atomic" to "Hydrogen." In a sense, for the the political cartoonist to take on the problem of nuclear bombs and their increasing numbers is really a question of knocking down a straw man. Who has seen a cartoon in *support* of nuclear proliferation? One even wonders how a cartoonist with that in mind would design such a notion on his drawing board. Would the bomb look like a Defender of the Faith or the Statue of Liberty?

It is an old truism that the gruesome and the funny are very close. Here, though, because of the truly diabolical nature of the subject at hand, it is not to be funny that the contributing cartoonists have delivered their treatments. They are well aware that it is the most serious work that any of them will ever do.

GEORGE PLIMPTON

1.

2.

"Forgive me for the horrible thing I have done."

3.

5.

"Forgive me for the horrible thing I have done."

6.

4.

7.

BOOTH

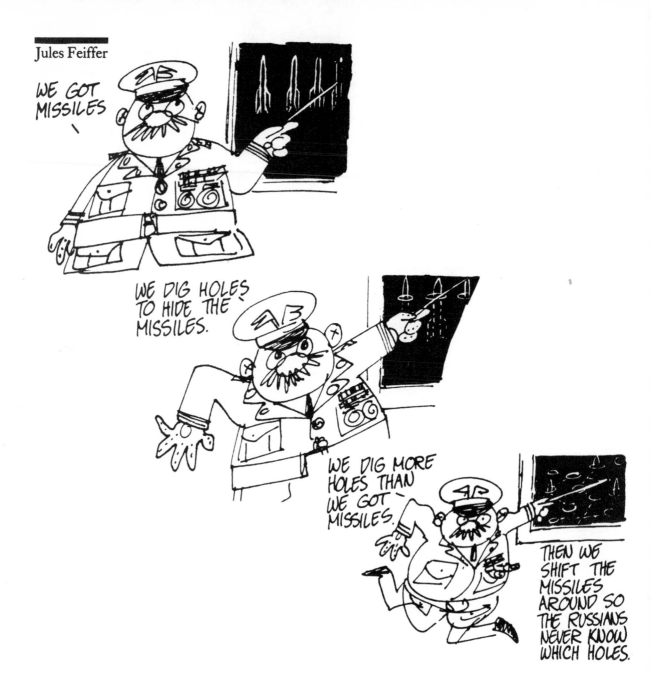

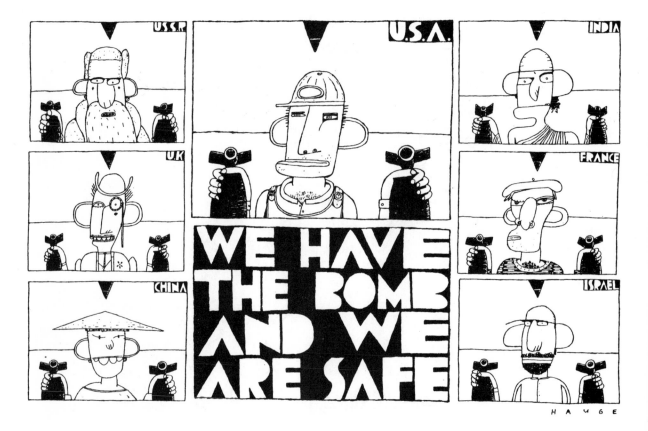

"Oops!"

17

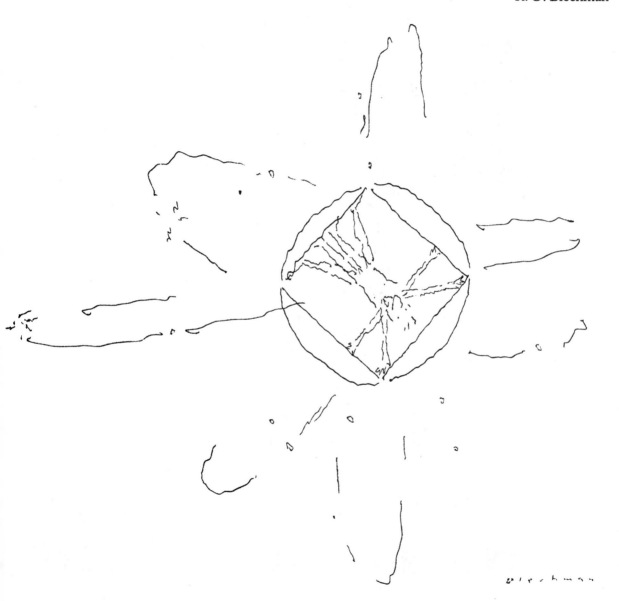

blechman

19

Brad Holland

Bogey

Jules Stauber

Philip Burke

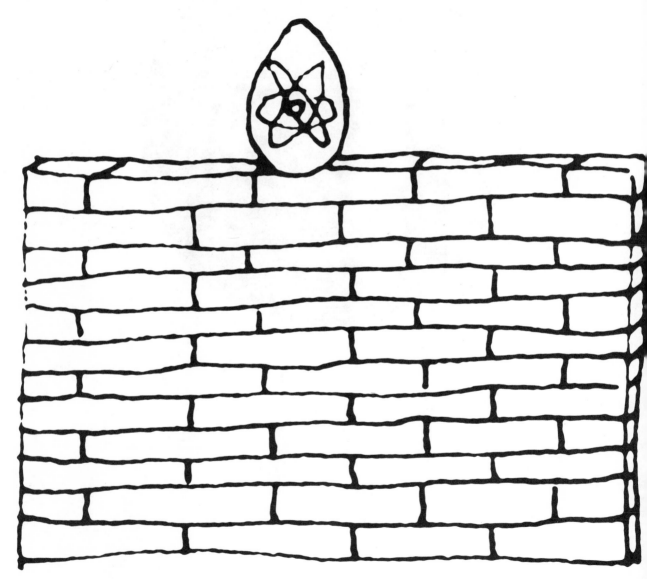

Andrzej
Dudzinski

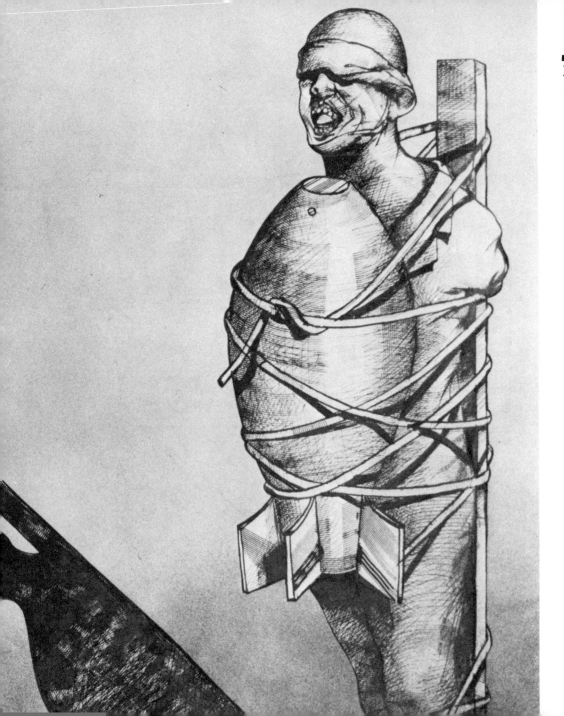

Marshall
Arisman

Lee Lorenz

"As I see it, our commitment to the peace process is only credible if our commitment to the war process is credible."

33

Michael Maslin

"What do you mean, 'What war?'"

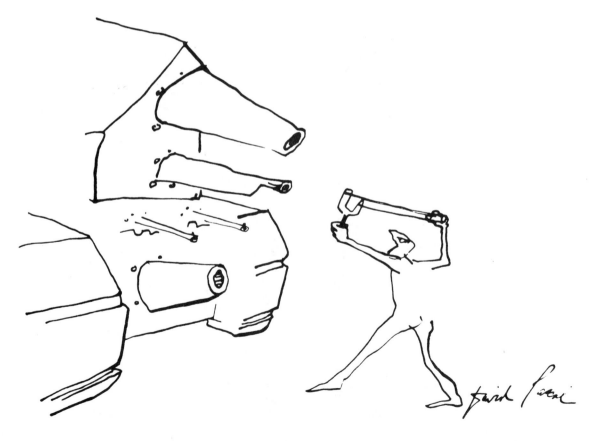

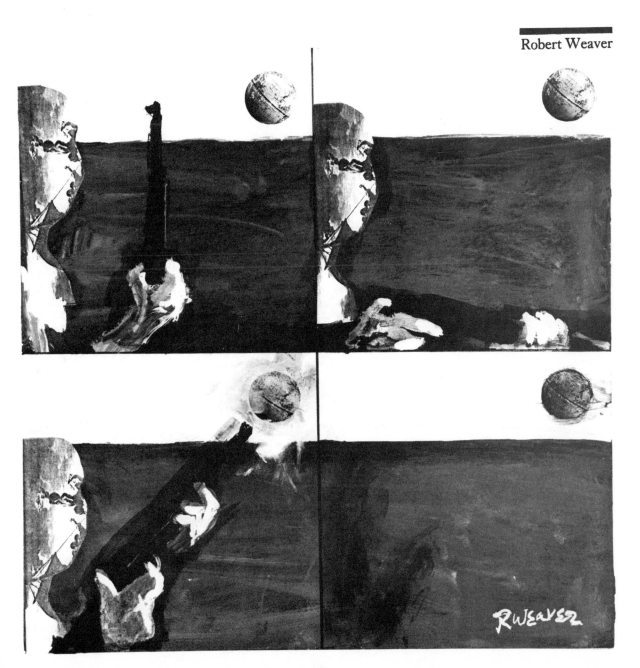

41

Jack Ziegler

"And you call yourself a nuclear physicist??"

43

the Nebbishes

The world can't come to an end because I'm too busy.

Gardner

*"One consolation - if there is a nuclear war, we won't have
to hear about it every two seconds on radio and TV."*

Robert Grossman

THE HUMAN RACE

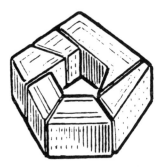

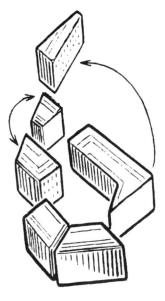

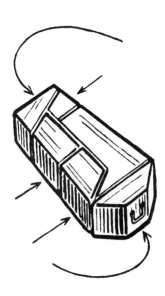

Mark Alan Stamaty

Edward Koren

Niculae Asciu

Mick Stevens

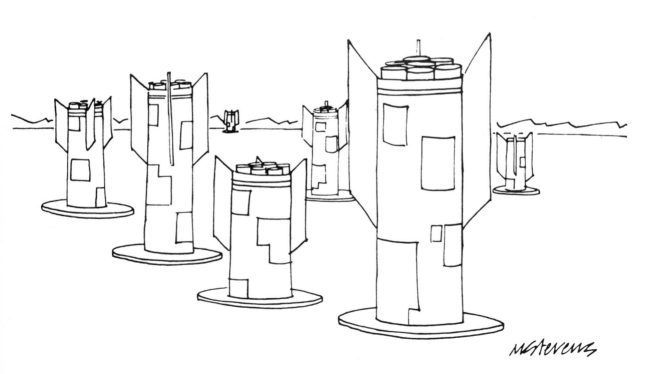

Eugene
Mihaesco

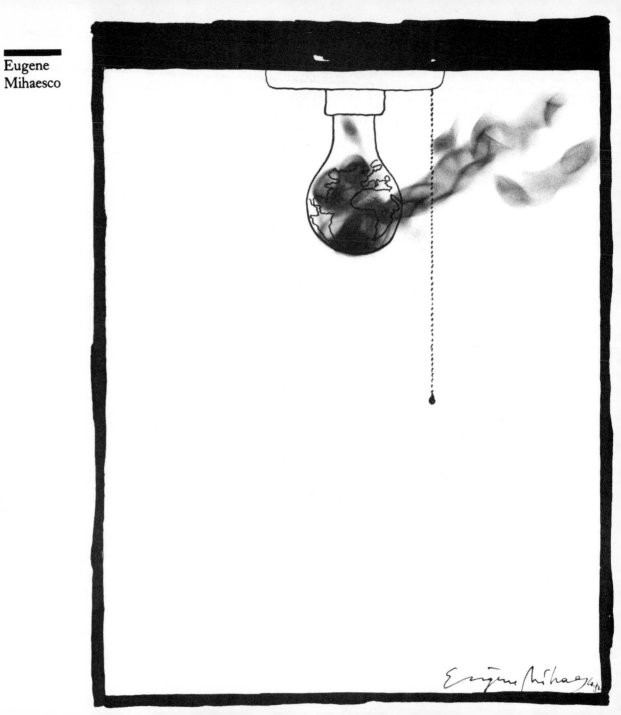

Frances Jetter

A Fun-Loving U.N. Considers Nuclear Disarmament

Gerald Scarfe

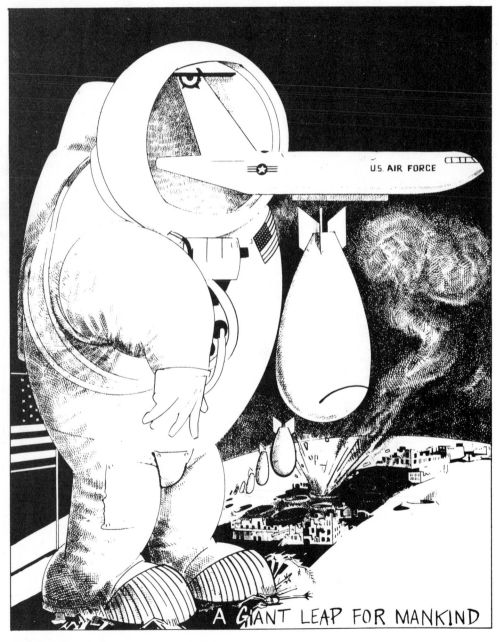

Fritz Eichenberg

William Garner

David Suter

67

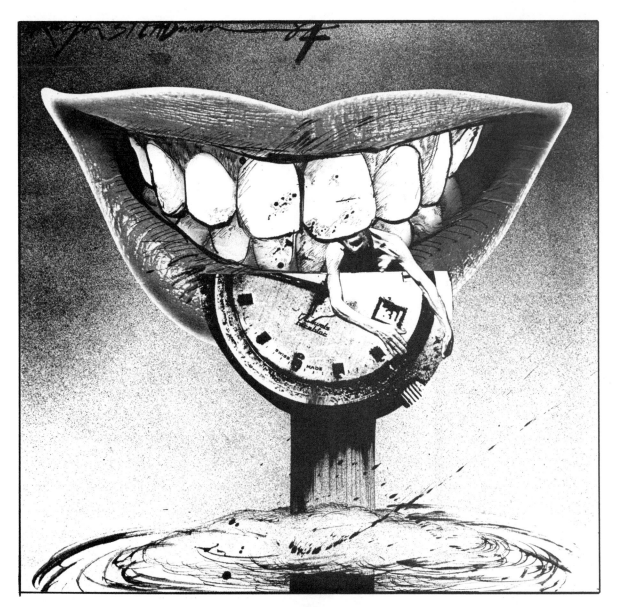

RELAX... WE'VE GOT 30 SECONDS TILL THE HEAT WAVE HITS TO FOLLOW THESE NEW REAGAN CIVIL DEFENSE EVACUATION PROCEDURES...

Seymour Chwast

Paul Szep

No freeze on nuclear warheads — Reagan

"I'M NOT STOPPING UNTIL I CATCH UP WITH HIM!"

Mark Alan Stamaty

WASHINGTOON   ©1982 BY MARK ALAN STAMATY

Like most perceptions, it was first detected as a sense by a perceptographer in the Senses Bureau.

There is a rapidly growing sense that the President is pursuing a dangerous policy with regard to nuclear arms.

Immediately Perceiver General Hotwall was notified.

Looks like trouble... we've got to diffuse it before it becomes a perception!

BZZZNN!

PERCEPT

UH-OH!

It just did.

As his staff swung into action, tracking and charting the new perception, Hotwall began giving orders.

Get me THE WHITE HOUSE... and the Office of Lip Service!...

The next day he met with the President and told him of the perception.

How bad is it, Bayard? Could it damage my prestige?

Well... it's serious, but I think we can neutralize it. I've got some ideas...

Later that week the President gave his first address to the nation on the subject of nuclear disarmament:

We must establish a dialogue with the Soviets.

For this purpose, I will appoint a team of our finest meteorologists to meet in Geneva with their Soviet counterparts and begin comprehensive discussions of the weather.

We will call these talks STALL -Strategic Arms Limitation Limbo.

The STALL talks will continue until we win the arms race, at which time we will appoint a team of interior designers to begin negotiations on the shape of the bargaining table

During the weeks that followed, Bayard kept a close watch on the unwanted perception

Has it diminished yet?

Not much.

Not as much, for instance, as a certain perception of Bob Forehead.

He knows a lot more than I thought he did!

to be continued

78

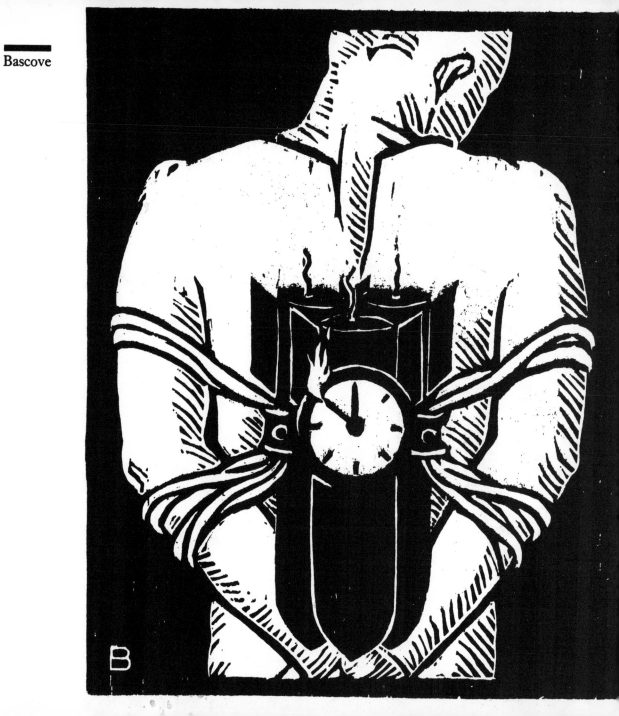

Bascove

'OUT OF THE WAY, YOU COMMIE NUISANCE — ER, NOT YOU, LEONID...THIS OTHER GUY!'

Luis Geronimo

'ARE YOU FINDING IT HARD TO CONCENTRATE?'

THE NUCLEAR CLOCK

NUCLEAR BOMB PRESS

THE DE-CREATION OF MAN BY REAGAN
APOLOGIES TO MICHELANGELO, AND WALT DISNEY
AND MANKIND.

89

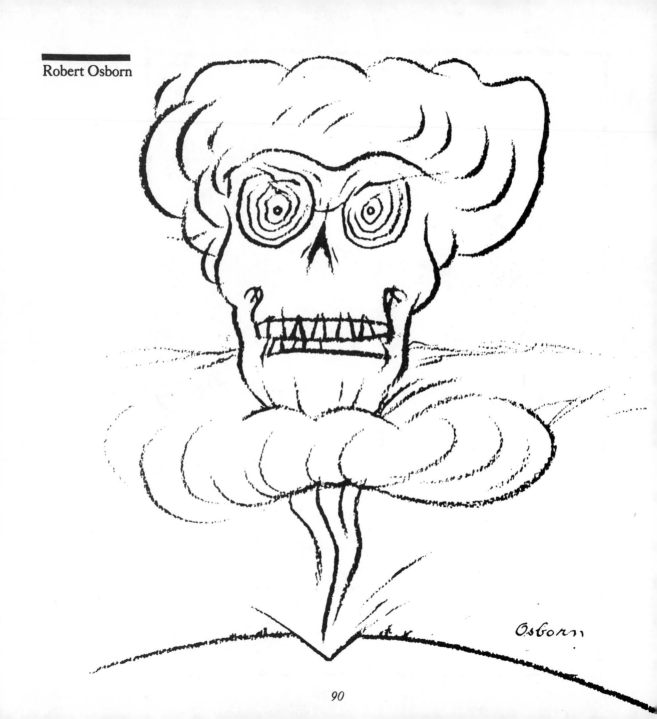

Osborn

Contributors

Julian Allen *(page 33)*
Illustrations appear in *Esquire*, the *Sunday Times* (London), *Rolling Stone*, and *The New York Times*.

Marshall Arisman *(page 24)*
Illustrations appear in *Playboy, Omni, Mother Jones*, and *The New York Times*. Contributor to *The Nation*. Has published *Frozen Images*, a collection of drawings.

Niculae Asciu *(page 54)*
Illustrations and cartoons appear in *The New York Times* and *The New Yorker*.

Tony Auth *(page 77)*
Pulitzer Prize - winning cartoonist for the *Philadelphia Inquirer*.

Bascove *(page 80)*
Illustrations appear in *Esquire, The New York Times*, and on book jackets.

R. O. Blechman *(page 19)*
Cartoons and illustrations appear in *The New York Times, Atlantic Monthly*, and many other periodicals. Animator and director of the Ink Tank Studio. Has published *Behind the Lines*, a retrospective of his work.

George Booth *(page 9)*
Regular contributor to *The New Yorker* and author of many books.

Philip Burke *(page 22)*
Caricatures appear in the *Village Voice*. Co-editor of the *New York Illustrated News*.

Seymour Chwast *(page 73)*
Co-proprietor of Pushpin, Lubalin, Peckolick design studio. Illustrations appear in numerous periodicals and books.

Sue Coe *(page 70)*
Drawings appear in *Esquire, Weekend, Mother Jones, The New York Times*, and other periodicals. Has had three solo exhibitions in Great Britain.

Paul Conrad *(page 84)*
Pulitzer Prize - winning cartoonist for the *Los Angeles Times*.

R. Crumb *(page 43)*
Creator of *Mr. Natural* and *Fritz the Cat*. Works appear in *Co-Evolution Quarterly* and *Weirdo*.

Andrzej Dudzinski *(page 23)*
Illustrations appear in *The New York Times, Harper's, Atlantic Monthly*, and other periodicals.

Fritz Eichenberg *(page 62)*
Founding director of the Pratt Graphic Center. Has illustrated more than a hundred books. A regular contributor to the *Catholic Worker*, among other periodicals.

Jules Feiffer *(page 12)*
Syndicated cartoonist whose work has appeared weekly in the *Village Voice* for twenty-six years. An anthology of cartoons, *Jules Feiffer's America: From Eisenhower to Reagan*, was recently published.

Peter Fluck and Roger Law *(front cover)*
Their three-dimensional caricatures have appeared in the *Sunday Times Magazine* (London), *Stern*, and many other magazines in Europe and the United States. They are presently producing a satirical, animated weekly series for the BBC.

Herb Gardner *(page 44)*
Playwright *(A Thousand Clowns, Thieves, The Goodbye People)*, screenwriter, short story writer, and creator of *The Nebbishes*.

William Garner *(page 64)*
Editorial cartoonist for the *Memphis* (Tennessee) *Commercial Appeal*.

Luis Geronimo *(page 82)*
Editorial cartoonist for *El Heraldo* (Mexico City).

Lou Grant *(page 48)*
Editorial cartoonist for the *Oakland* (California) *Tribune*.

Sam Gross *(page 35)*
Cartoons appear in *The New Yorker* and *National Lampoon*. A cartoon collection, *More Gross*, was recently published.

Robert Grossman *(page 46)*
Illustrator, cartoonist, and animator. Works appear in *The New York Times, Time, Newsweek,* and other periodicals. *Zoo Nooz,* a comic strip, ran in *New York* and *Rolling Stone.*

Ron Hauge *(page 14)*
Cartoons appear in *The Progressive* and *National Lampoon.*

Draper Hill *(page 87)*
Editorial cartoonist for the *Detroit News.* Author of a biography of James Gilray.

Cor Hoekstra (CORK) *(page 63)*
Cartoons appear in *Suddeutsche Zeitung* (Munich) and the *World Press Review.*

Brad Holland *(page 20)*
Illustrations appear in numerous magazines and newspapers including *Newsweek, Time, The New York Times, Atlantic Monthly,* and the *Cleveland Plain Dealer.* Published *Human Scandals,* a collection of his drawings.

Frances Jetter *(page 58)*
Illustrations appear in *The Nation, The New York Times,* the *Village Voice,* and other publications. Founding member of INX, the graphic arts syndicate.

Edward Koren *(page 51)*
Regular contributor to *The New York-

er.* Illustrations and cartoons appear in *The Nation, The New York Times, Newsweek,* and other publications. Numerous collections of drawings, including *The Penguin Edward Koren.*

Stephen Kroninger *(page 36)*
Illustrations appear in the *Village Voice, New York Rocker,* and *Meat.*

Harvey Kurtzman *(page 26)*
Founding editor of *Mad, Trump, Humbug,* and *Help.*

Bill Lee *(page 41)*
Humor editor of *Penthouse.* Cartoons appear in *Penthouse, Omni,* and other publications. Co-editor of *Positively No Personnel Beyond This Point,* an anti-Vietnam War cartoon anthology.

David Levine *(pages 75, 96)*
Literary and political caricatures appear regularly in the *New York Review of Books* and *Esquire,* among other publications. Most recent collection is titled *The Arts of David Levine.*

M. G. Lord *(pages 79, 86)*
Editorial cartoonist for Long Island's *Newsday.* Most recent collection of drawings is titled *Mean Sheets.*

Lee Lorenz *(page 27)*
Art editor of *The New Yorker.* Cartoons appear regularly there and in other publications. He has illustrated numerous books.

Stan Mack *(page 52)*
Real Life Funnies appears weekly in the *Village Voice.*

Mark Marek *(page 68)*
Comic strips appear regularly in *National Lampoon.*

Doug Marlette *(page 76)*
Editorial cartoonist for the *Charlotte* (North Carolina) *Observer.* Creator of *Kudzo,* a comic strip.

Charles E. Martin *(page 17)*
Cartoons appear regularly in *The New Yorker* and other publications. One-man exhibitions at the Brooklyn Museum and the Graham Galleries in New York City.

Henry Martin *(page 45)*
Cartoons appear regularly in *The New Yorker* and other publications.

Michael Maslin *(page 34)*
Cartoons appear in *The New Yorker, National Lampoon,* and *Penthouse.*

Eugene Mihaesco *(page 56)*
Illustrations appear in *Time, The New York Times,* and on the cover of *The New Yorker.* One-man exhibition at the St. Etienne Gallery in New York City.

Lou Myers *(page 66)*
Cartoons and illustrations appear in many publications including *The New Yorker, The New York Times, Upper and Lower Case,* and *The Nation.* His

short stories appear in *The New Yorker*.

Pat Oliphant *(pages 81, 83)*
Pulitzer Prize - winning cartoonist for the *Denver Post* and the *Washington Star*. Syndicated in more than three hundred newspapers and a contributor to *Time*.

Robert Osborn *(pages 5, 65, 90)*
Drawings have appeared in the *New Republic*, *Harper's*, and many other journals, books, and periodicals. Most recent book is *Osborn on Osborn*.

David Pascal *(page 38)*
Organizer of the First American International Comics Congress. Cartoons appear in *The New Yorker*, *The New York Times*, *Punch*, and others.

Mike Peters *(page 72)*
Pulitzer Prize - winning cartoonist for the *Dayton* (Ohio) *News*. Cartoons are syndicated in more than three hundred newspapers.

Bill Plympton
(back cover and page 88)
Cartoons are syndicated by Universal Press Syndicate.

Mark Podwal *(page 37)*
Illustrations appear in *The New York Times*. Author of numerous visual books, including *Freud's Da Vinci*.

Ken Pyne *(page 28)*
Cartoonist for *Punch* and other publications in England.

Hans Georg Rauch *(page 61)*
Cartoonist and illustrator whose work has appeared in periodicals throughout Europe and the United States, including *Stern*, *Pardon*, *Harper's*, and *The New York Times*. His recent collection of drawings is *Battlelines*.

Mischa Richter *(page 91)*
Contributor to *The New Yorker* and other publications and has illustrated many books.

Arnold Roth *(page 59)*
Contributor to numerous periodicals including *The New York Times*, *Punch*, *The Nation*, and *The Progressive*. Has illustrated many books.

Ben Sargent *(page 57)*
Pulitzer Prize - winning editorial cartoonist for the *American - Statesman* newspaper (Austin, Texas).

Gerald Scarfe *(pages 60, 85)*
Cartoonist, animator, and illustrator. Drawings appear regularly in *The Times* (London). Most recent film is *The Wall*.

Ronald Searle *(page 89)*
Cartoonist, satirist, illustrator, and historian. His recent collection of drawings is titled *Ronald Searle*.

Elwood H. Smith *(pages 1, 29)*
Cartoons and illustrations appear in *Esquire*, *Rolling Stone*, *New York*, and numerous other periodicals.

Edward Sorel *(page 32)*
Winner of the Polk Award for satiric drawing. Cartoons appear in numerous magazines. A regular contributor to *Atlantic Monthly*. Most recent collection of drawings is titled *Superpen*.

Mark Alan Stamaty *(pages 50, 78)*
Comic strip, *Washingtoon*, appears weekly in the *Washington Post* and the *Village Voice*. Most recent book is *MacDoodle Street*.

Jules Stauber *(page 21)*
Editorial cartoonist for *Nebelspalter* (Zurich).

Ralph Steadman *(page 69)*
Graphic satires appear in *Rolling Stone*, *Penthouse*, *The New York Times*, and others. Books include *America* and *Sigmund Freud*.

Peter Steiner *(pages 3, 53)*
Cartoons appear in *The New Yorker* and *National Lampoon*.

Mick Stevens *(page 55)*
Cartoons appear in *The New Yorker* and *National Lampoon*.

David Suter *(pages 49, 67)*
Illustrations appear in *The New York*

Times, Time, Harper's, and *Atlantic Monthly,* among others.

Paul Szep *(page 74)*
Pulitzer Prize - winning cartoonist for the *Boston Globe.* Recently published collection of cartoons is titled *Warts and All.*

Roland Topor *(page 18)*
Work has appeared in *The New York Times, Scanlan's,* and other American and European publications. Has published more than thirty books in Europe, including *Toxology.*

John Trever *(page 40)*
Editorial cartoonist for the *Albuquerque* (New Mexico) *Journal.*

Garry Trudeau *(page 30)*
Pulitzer Prize - winning creator of *Doonesbury.* Strip is syndicated in more than four hundred newspapers. Has published numerous anthologies.

Robert Weaver *(page 39)*
Illustrator whose work has appeared on posters, in books, and in many publications, including *New York, The New York Times, Time, Life,* and *Audience.* Teaches at the School of Visual Arts, New York City.

Gahan Wilson *(page 16)*
A regular contributor to *Playboy.* Cartoons appear in *The New Yorker, The New York Times,* and many other publications. Has published many anthologies. Commentator for National Public Radio.

Don Wright *(page 15)*
Pulitzer Prize - winning cartoonist for the *Miami Herald.* Most recent collection titled *Wright On.*

Jack Ziegler *(page 42)*
Regular contributor to *The New Yorker, National Lampoon,* and other publications. Most recent collection of cartoons is titled *Filthy Little Things.*

Steven Heller *(editor)*
Author of *Man Bites Man: Two Decades of Satiric Art 1960-80* and editor of *Jules Feiffer's America: From Eisenhower to Reagan,* among others.

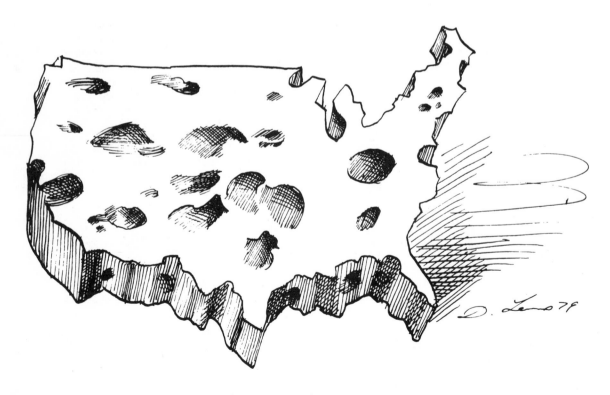